The Liberty Bell

by Judith Jango-Cohen

Lerner Publications Company • Minneapolis

To Susan Rose, an editor any writer would be lucky to have

This book is available in two editions:
Library binding by Lerner Publications Company, a division of Lerner Publishing Group
Soft cover by First Avenue Editions, an imprint of Lerner Publishing Group
241 First Avenue North
Minneapolis, MN 55401 U.S.A.

Website address: www.lernerbooks.com

Words in **bold type** are explained in a glossary on page 31.

Library of Congress Cataloging-in-Publication Data

Jango-Cohen, Judith.
     The Liberty Bell / by Judith Jango-Cohen.
         p.   cm. – (Pull ahead books)
     Includes index.
     Summary: An introduction to the history of the Liberty Bell.
     ISBN-13: 978–0–8225–3803–5 (lib. bdg. : alk. paper)
     ISBN-10: 0–8225–3803–2 (lib. bdg. : alk. paper)
     ISBN-13: 978–0–8225–3754–0 (pbk. : alk. paper)
     ISBN-10: 0–8225–3754–0 (pbk. : alk. paper)
     1. Liberty Bell–Juvenile literature. 2. Philadelphia (Pa.)–
Buildings, structures, etc.–Juvenile literature. [1. Liberty
Bell.] I. Title. II. Series.
     F158.8.I3 J36 2004
     974.8'11–dc21   2002013947

Manufactured in the United States of America
3 4 5 6 7 8 – JR – 11 10 09 08 07 06

Philadelphia, Pennsylvania, was a busy city in the 1750s. What were the sounds in this city?

Horses clomped. People talked in little
brick shops. And a big clanging bell
rang in the **State House.**

Words on the bell read, "Proclaim **liberty** throughout all the land." Liberty is another word for freedom.

This bell is a **symbol** that stands for liberty. It is called the Liberty Bell.

In 1752, the bell had just come on a ship from England. On the very first ring, it cracked!

John Pass and John Stow fixed the cracked bell. They melted it down to liquid metal. They added some **copper** to make it stronger.

Pass and Stow poured the metal into a mold. They **cast** a new bell. It was a big, clanging, bonging bell.

Ben Franklin was one of Philadelphia's leaders. He listened to all the clanging, clomping, and talking. What sound did he like best?

Ben said, "The sweetest of all sounds is liberty." But how can you hear liberty?

Ben heard liberty in the sounds of people praying. In Pennsylvania, people were free to pray in their own way.

Most people in Pennsylvania had come from other countries. In these countries, kings told the people how to pray.

Ben also heard liberty at meetings in the State House. People were free to say what they thought.

In some countries, people went to jail if the king didn't like what they said.

England ruled America in the 1750s. The Liberty Bell rang when there was news from England.

People gathered to hear new laws that England made. Americans did not like England's laws. They wanted to be free to make their own laws.

Ben Franklin went to talk to England's leaders. The Liberty Bell rang out to wish him well.

But Ben could not make England's leaders understand. People in America grew angry.

They decided to go to war for their
freedom.

In 1776, Thomas Jefferson wrote the **Declaration of Independence.** It declared that America was free from England. America was **independent.**

The Liberty Bell called out the news on July 8, 1776. It proclaimed liberty throughout all the land.

"Huzzah! Huzzah!" people cheered.
"God bless the free states of America!"

Seventy years later, the Liberty Bell
was still ringing. It rang for George
Washington's birthday.

Then a small crack grew into a big one. The Liberty Bell could not ring again.

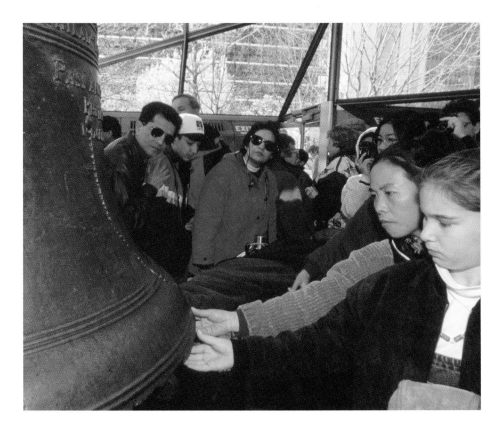

Still, the Liberty Bell is important to Americans. People come to Philadelphia to see and touch this bell.

Now the old bell is a silent symbol. It is a symbol of liberty, the sweetest sound of all.

Facts about the Liberty Bell

■ Pennsylvania is spelled "Pensylvania" on the Liberty Bell. This is an old spelling that is no longer used.

■ The Pass and Stow bell was hung in the State House in 1753. But people did not like the sound of the bell. So Pass and Stow cast a second bell. This is the Liberty Bell we know today.

■ In 1772, people living near the State House complained to Pennsylvania's leaders. They were upset about "the too frequent ringing by the great bell in the steeple."

■ British soldiers melted bells that they captured during the war. They used the metal for musket shot and cannon balls. Americans removed the Liberty Bell before the British entered Philadelphia in 1777. The bell was hidden under the floor of a church in Allentown, Pennsylvania.

■ The Liberty Bell no longer hangs in the State House. It is on display in a glass building nearby.

Travels of the Liberty Bell

The Liberty Bell has not spent all its time in Pennsylvania. Between 1885 and 1915, it traveled 25,000 miles around the country. It visited almost 400 cities on seven different trips. Cheering crowds greeted the Liberty Bell with flags, flowers, and parades.

1885– to New Orleans, Louisiana

1893– to Chicago, Illinois

1895– to Atlanta, Georgia

1902– to Charleston, South Carolina

1903– to Boston, Massachusetts

1904– to St. Louis, Missouri

1915– to San Francisco, California

There are no more trips planned for the Liberty Bell. Moving the old bell could damage it. But each year, one and a half million people visit the bell in its Philadelphia home.

More about the Liberty Bell

Books

Aliki. *The Many Lives of Benjamin Franklin.* Englewood Cliffs, NJ: Prentice-Hall, 1977.

Giblin, James Cross. *Thomas Jefferson.* New York: Scholastic, 1994.

Marzollo, Jean. *In 1776.* New York: Scholastic, 1994.

Slate, Joseph. *The Great Big Wagon that Rang: How the Liberty Bell Was Saved.* Tarrytown, NY: Marshall Cavendish, 2002.

Websites

The Declaration of Independence
http://www.ushistory.org/declaration/

Independence National Historical Park
http://www.independencevisitorcenter.com

Liberty Bell Shrine
http://www.fieldtrip.com/pa/04354232.htm

Liberty Bell Virtual Museum
http://www.libertybellmuseum.com/

Visiting the Liberty Bell

The Liberty Bell is at the Liberty Bell Center at Independence National Historical Park in Philadelphia, Pennsylvania. The park is open year-round.

Glossary

cast: to pour liquid metal into a mold. The hardened metal takes the shape of the mold.

copper: a reddish-brown metal that is easily shaped

Declaration of Independence: the statement declaring that America had the right to be free from Great Britain.

independent: free from the control of other people or another country

liberty: freedom to act, speak, and believe as you choose

State House: the meeting place for the leaders of Pennsylvania

symbol: an object that stands for an idea, a country, or a person

Index

crack, 7–8, 25

England, 7, 16–19

Franklin, Ben, 10–12, 14, 18–19

independence, 21–23

Jefferson, Thomas, 21

liberty, 5–6, 11–12, 14, 22, 27

Pass, John, 8–9
Pennsylvania, 3, 12–13
Philadelphia, 3–4, 10, 26

sounds, 3–4, 10–12, 14, 27
State House, 4, 14
Stow, John, 8–9
symbol, 6, 27

war, 20
Washington, George, 24

Photo Acknowledgments

The pictures in this book have been reproduced with the permission of: © North Wind Picture Archive, pp. 3, 12, 13, 15, 16, 17, 21, 23; © Hulton|Archive by Getty Images, pp. 4, 24; © A.A.M. Van der Heyden/Independent Pictures Service, p. 5; Library of Congress, pp. 6 (LC-USZC2-212), 14 (LC-USZC2-2452), 20 (LC-USZ62-96106), 22 (LC-USZC2-729); © Historic Urban Plans, p. 7; Diderot Pictorial Encyclopedia of Trades and Industry, p. 8; SuperStock, pp. 9, 19; Independent Picture Service, p. 10; National Archives (W&C 65), p. 11; © Huntington Library/Superstock, p. 18; © Bob Krist/CORBIS, p. 25; © Robert Homes/CORBIS, p. 26; © Leif Skoogfors/CORBIS, p. 27.

Cover photograph used with the permission of © Leif Skoogfors/CORBIS.